DANGEROUS

Adventures
in the Air

SIMON LEWIS

W
FRANKLIN WATTS
LONDON•SYDNEY

An Appleseed Editions book

First published in 2008 by Franklin Watts

Paperback edition 2009

Franklin Watts
338 Euston Road, London NW1 3BH

Franklin Watts Australia
Hachette Children's Books
Level 17/207 Kent St, Sydney, NSW 2000

2008 Appleseed Editions

Appleseed Editions Ltd
Well House, Friars Hill, Guestling, East Sussex TN35 4ET

Created by Q2AMedia
Series Editor: Jean Coppendale; Book Editor: Paul Manning
Senior Art Designers: Ashita Murgai, Nishant Mudgal
Designers: Diksha Khatri, Shilpi Sarkar; Picture Researcher: Lalit Dalal
Line Artists: Amit Tayal, Sibi N.D
Illustrators: Aadil Ahmed Siddiqui, Amir Khan, Manish Prasad, Sanyogita Lal, Vijay Sharma

ISBN 978 0 7496 9282 7

Dewey classification: 327.12

All words in **bold** can be found in the glossary on page 30.

Website information is correct at time of going to press. However, the publishers cannot
accept liability for any information or links found on third-party websites.

A CIP catalogue for this book is available from the British Library.

Picture credits
t=top b=bottom c=centre l=left r=right m=middle
Cover: Q2AMedia
Bettmann/ Corbis: 4, Sheila Terry/ SPL/ Photolibrary: 5t, Richard Cooke/ Alamy: 5b, PPL Ltd/ Rex Features: 6t,
A Henry/ AWM: 9, Lindbergh Picture Collection. Manuscripts & Archives, Yale University Library: 11,
The Print Collector/ Alamy: 15, Corbis: 16t, Popperfoto/ Alamy: 19t, Bettmann/ Corbis: 20t,
Purdue University Libraries, Archives and Special Collections: 20b, AF.MIL: 21, JPL/ NASA: 23l, 23r,
AF.MIL: 25, Virgin Atlantic Global Flyer: 26, 27tb, 28

Printed in China

Franklin Watts is a division of Hachette Children's Books,
an Hachette UK company.
www.hachette.co.uk

DIFFICULT & DANGEROUS

Adventures in the Air

SIMON LEWIS

W
FRANKLIN WATTS
LONDON · SYDNEY

REACHING FOR THE SKIES

From earliest times, people have dreamed of conquering the skies. Today, travelling by plane is no more difficult or dangerous than going by train or car. But it wasn't always so. The history of aviation is full of men and women who risked their lives in order to fly higher, faster and further than human beings had ever flown before.

The first aviators

In early times people tried to fly like birds by attaching wings to their arms. It was not until 1903, when the Wright brothers in America combined cleverly crafted wings on a wooden frame with a lightweight petrol engine, that the world's first powered aeroplane, the *Kitty Hawk*, took to the skies. On 17 December, the brothers made three flights, the longest lasting 59 seconds. Six years later, French pilot Louis Blériot flew the English Channel for the first time.

*The Wright brothers, Orville and Wilbur, were the first to achieve a successful flight in a heavier-than-air **fixed-wing** aircraft.*

The dream of flight

In early times, people tried to fly by imitating the flapping motion of a bird's wings. This sketch by the artist and inventor Leonardo da Vinci was made in about 1488. It shows an artificial wing being moved rapidly up and down by means of a lever.

Flying fighters

The first main use of aeroplanes was in warfare. In World War I, the German flying ace Baron von Richthofen (see page 6) showed how deadly fighter planes could be. Later, pilots such as Americans Charles Lindbergh and Amelia Earhart used their skills and courage to make ever longer and more dangerous flights. Bigger and better planes were being built all the time. Even today aviators are testing human endurance and technology to the limits.

Displays by skilled aerobatics teams such as the RAF Red Arrows show the speed and agility of modern fighter planes.

THE RED BARON

Manfred von Richthofen

The German Baron Manfred von Richthofen (1891-1918) was the most successful fighter pilot of World War I. He became known as the 'Red Baron' because he flew a bright red Fokker triplane. In only 20 months, Richthofen shot down 80 Allied aircraft. The sight of Richthofen's red plane was enough to strike terror in the hearts of Allied fighter pilots.

One of the most highly skilled and feared of all flying aces, the Red Baron received 24 military decorations for his services.

Western Front

GREAT BRITAIN

● London

GERMANY

Cambrai

BELGIUM

Paris ●

FRANCE

Map of the Western Front in 1916 showing Cambrai in Occupied France, where the Red Baron scored his first victory.

The first kill

Richthofen began his career with the German air force in the early days of World War I. After only 21 hours' training, he made his first solo flight - and crash-landed! But soon his flying exploits so impressed his superiors that he was chosen to fly with the Germans' top unit, Jagdstaffel 2. On 1 September 1916, Richthofen reported for duty on the Western Front. Soon after, he shot down his first enemy plane over Cambrai, France.

> "... He knew exactly that his last hour had arrived at the moment when I got at the back of him. At that time I had not yet the conviction 'He must fall!' which I have now on such occasions ..."
>
> Baron von Richthofen describing his first kill in his autobiography, The Red Battle Flyer (1917)

The Red Baron closes in on his prey during a fierce **dogfight** over the Western Front.

Richthofen leads his unit, Jagdgeschwader 1, on a combat mission. The unit was nick-named the 'Flying Circus' because of the bright colours of the planes and the large circus-like tents where the pilots and their machines were housed.

Circus of death

By January 1917, Richthofen had destroyed 16 enemy planes and was a national hero. The German **High Command** even tried to prevent him flying in order to protect him from injury. But nothing could keep the Red Baron away from the action. On 29 April, he shot down four planes in one day - a personal best - and reached an all-time record of 41 enemy planes shot down in total.

The Baron's last flight

In July 1917, Richthofen was shot down by an English plane. Despite a bullet wound to the head, he survived and was soon back in the air. On 1 September he shot down his sixtieth plane. Then, on 21 April 1918, the Red Baron began his last, fatal flight. During a fierce dogfight, a Canadian pilot dived on the Baron's blood-red Fokker from above, while Australian soldiers on the ground fired from below. Richthofen's plane was hit. The Australians recovered the plane and the body of the greatest combat pilot ever known. The reign of the Red Baron was over.

A postcard of the time shows Australian servicemen removing the body of the Red Baron from the wreckage of his Fokker triplane.

Who killed the Red Baron?

Richthofen died of a bullet wound to the chest. Various individuals claimed the honour of bringing him down, but no one knows for certain who fired the fatal shot.

Richthofen was buried in France with full military honours. Germany went into deep mourning at the loss of their hero. In 1925, his body was taken back to Germany and given the largest funeral ever seen in Berlin.

9

Master of the skies

Before joining the air force, Richthofen had been a keen huntsman, and had learned skills that were vital for aerial combat. As a pilot, he loved the thrill of the chase, was quick-thinking, stuck to his target and fired fast. He was also a master of tactics such as diving 'out of the sun' or swooping under an enemy plane to fire at it from below.

German pilots had no parachutes: it was thought to encourage cowardice if they could ditch their planes to get out of trouble!

The German Fokker planes were fast and agile. But they had one big drawback: the Lewis gun mounted on the fuselage could only be fired forwards or upwards – it did not swivel round like the guns of the British Sopwith Camels. This left the pilot very exposed.

How would YOU survive?

1 Which of these qualities would you need to survive an encounter with the deadly Red Baron?

Nerves of steel	Ruthlessness	Decisiveness
Sharp eyes	Calmness	Fear of heights
Team spirit	Honesty	Lightning reflexes
Friendliness	Easy-going nature	Reckless courage

2 If you had a choice, which plane would you rather fly, a Fokker or a Sopwith Camel?

Fokker
Guns could only fire upwards or forwards
Could climb quickly
Easy to control

Sopwith Camel
Guns could turn from side to side
Faster than the Fokker
Could easily spin out of control

A PASSION FOR PLANES

Charles Lindbergh's solo transatlantic flight

*Born in Detroit in 1902, Charles Lindbergh always had a passion for planes. As a young man, he trained as a pilot, bought a plane of his own and even took a job as a **stunt flyer**.*

It was while working as an airmail delivery pilot that Lindbergh heard of a prize of $25,000 being offered for the first person to fly non-stop from New York to Paris. Nothing like this had ever been attempted. It was a challenge an adventurer such as Lindbergh could not resist.

The journey of a lifetime

Deciding to fly single-handed so as to be able to carry more fuel, Lindbergh planned the flight to the last detail. By 28 April 1927, his plane, *Spirit of St Louis*, had been designed and built to meet his exact requirements. After short test flights, he set out from San Diego to Long Island, a distance nearly equal to that from New York to Paris. He made it in 21 hours 20 minutes, setting a new coast-to-coast record. He was ready to begin the journey of his life.

Once dubbed 'the flying fool' because of his reckless courage, Charles Lindbergh (1902–74) is recognized today as one of the great pioneers of aviation.

Alone in mid-Atlantic

On the morning of 20 May 1927, a crowd of 500 gathered to watch the *Spirit of St Louis* take off from Roosevelt Field on Long Island. Spectators gasped as the plane, holding 1,707 litres of fuel, narrowly missed the **telegraph** wires and trees at the end of the dirt runway. Moments later Lindbergh had set course and was heading safely for the Atlantic. His historic flight was underway.

Storm ahead!

By the time Lindbergh reached Newfoundland, night was falling and storm clouds were gathering. Thick fog surrounded the plane, hiding the ocean from view. Fearing that ice would form on the cockpit and wings, Lindbergh struggled to avoid the storm and still stay on course. Tiredness was already setting in. Despite the freezing cold, he opened the cockpit windows to keep himself awake.

'The tops of the storm clouds were several thousand feet above me and at one time, when I attempted to fly through one of the larger clouds, sleet started to collect on the plane. I was forced to turn around and get back into clear air immediately.'

Charles Lindbergh,
The Spirit of St Louis (1953)

*Lashed by wind and freezing **sleet**, Lindbergh battles with the Atlantic storm clouds. Even today, ice is a deadly hazard for planes, limiting visibility, adding weight and reducing the flow of air over the wings.*

Saturday, 21 May 1927

By dawn the next morning, Lindbergh was once more enveloped in a thick bank of fog. The hours that followed were among the most difficult and dangerous of the flight. By 7.52 a.m. he had been airborne for 24 hours and was struggling to keep exhaustion at bay. Time and again he thought he could see shorelines in the distance, with trees outlined against the horizon. He wrote later: 'The **mirages** were so natural that, had I not been in mid-Atlantic and known that no land existed along my route, I would have taken them to be actual islands.'

Lindbergh: the facts

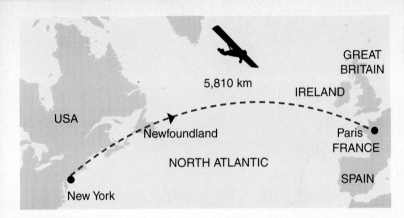

THE ROUTE
On paper, Lindbergh's route looks curved. In fact, his flight plan took advantage of the curve in the earth's surface to give him the shortest possible distance between New York and Paris.

THE PLANE
Inside *Spirit of St Louis*, the cockpit was so small that Lindbergh couldn't even stretch his legs. His only view was out of the side windows and via a **periscope** mounted on the left-hand side of the plane.

With so much space taken up by fuel tanks, Lindbergh only had room for the bare essentials. Here's what he took with him:

LINDBERGH'S EQUIPMENT LIST

2 torches	2 canteens
1 ball of string	1 cup
1 ball of cord	1 air raft with pump
1 hunting knife	
4 red flares	5 cans army rations
1 box of matches	
1 large needle	2 air cushions
	1 hacksaw blade

'Which way to Ireland?'

By morning, the skies had cleared. Lindbergh was over halfway to Paris. The bright sunshine revived him briefly, but soon tiredness overcame him again. He even fell asleep at the controls, but only for a moment.

At around 3 p.m., he saw fishing boats below. He circled low, yelling "Which way to Ireland?" but got no reply. Soon he saw the coast of Ireland and set course for France. By 10 p.m. he was flying over Paris. He circled the **Eiffel Tower**, then flew straight to the field at Le Bourget where he landed at 11.22 p.m. It had taken him 33 hours, 30 minutes and 29.5 seconds to travel non-stop from New York to Paris. He had done it!

Hero's welcome

Lindbergh was an instant hero on both sides of the Atlantic. On his return to New York thousands lined the streets to welcome him back. His epic flight had put aviation on the map. From now on, people began to take a greater interest in planes and what they could do.

*'It is the greatest shot of **adrenaline** to be doing what you have wanted to do so badly. You almost feel like you could fly without the plane.'*

Charles Lindbergh

When he saw fishing boats below, Lindbergh knew his goal was within reach. Less than an hour later the south-west coast of Ireland came into view.

Could YOU fly solo across the Atlantic?

Have you got what it takes to fly across the Atlantic alone, and without sleep for over 33 hours? Choose **A**, **B** or **C** from the questions below and then check your score.

A My favourite holiday is camping with lots of friends.
B I like going to museums and galleries.
C I like to go to the beach with my best friends.

A I love parties!
B I like to read or listen to music.
C I enjoy chatting with friends.

A My favourite lesson is sport.
B My favourite lesson is science.
C My favourite lesson is English.

A I get easily bored.
B I can always think of something to do.
C I like activities with lots of other people.

ANSWERS

Mostly As: You are active, like to be outdoors with lots of people. Spending time by yourself in a small plane would not be much fun for you.

Mostly Bs: You don't mind being alone and could find ways to keep yourself amused during a long, lonely flight at night.

Mostly Cs: You're one of the gang and enjoy being part of a team – perhaps you should stay on the ground!

VOYAGE OF MYSTERY
The last flight of Amelia Earhart

Kansas-born Amelia Earhart (1897-1937) was 12 years old before she even saw a plane and 20 before she took her first aeroplane flight. But from the moment the plane lifted her into the air, she was determined that she would one day become a pilot.

Amelia Earhart's daring and courage inspired many other women to live their dreams.

The ultimate challenge

In 1932, on the fifth anniversary of Lindbergh's transatlantic flight, the young aviator Amelia Earhart stormed into the record books, becoming the first woman - and only the second person - to fly solo across the Atlantic. Many other outstanding flying achievements followed. But at the age of 40, Earhart's greatest challenge still lay ahead of her: to fly around the world.

Earhart's Lockheed Elektra 10E takes off from Lae, New Guinea, on the final leg of her round-the-world flight.

Epic flight

Earhart's first attempt at a round-the-world flight was thwarted in March 1937 when a tyre of her plane blew at take-off. Her second began on 1 June when she and **navigator** Fred Noonan successfully took off from Miami in their Lockheed Elektra 10E, bound for South America.

The first leg of Earhart's epic flight took her across South America, Africa and South-East Asia. At midnight on 2 July, she and Fred Noonan took off from Lae in New Guinea for the final and most hazardous part of their journey - a 11,265 km flight over the Pacific. It was a journey that would end in one of the great mysteries of modern times.

'Not much more than a month ago I was on the other shore of the Pacific, looking westward. This evening, I looked eastward over the Pacific. In the fast-moving days which have intervened, the whole width of the world has passed behind us — except this broad ocean. I shall be glad when we have the hazards of its navigation behind us.'

Amelia Earhart, before take-off on the final stage of her flight

Earhart's flight plan

1 21 May 1937 Leaves Oakland California.

2 29 June Arrives Lae, New Guinea, 35,400 km from start.

3 2 July Leaves Lae for Howland Island. Never arrives.

4 4–5 July Faint distress signals received from Phoenix Islands.

Lost without trace

Earhart was aiming for Howland Island, a tiny speck in mid-Pacific, where a US **coastguard** boat, *Itasca*, was waiting to guide her in to land. About 1,300 km into the flight, a crackle over the radio told Earhart that the *Itasca* was in position and standing by. Earhart radioed back to acknowledge the message. But although the crew of the *Itasca* could hear Earhart's voice over the radio, it was clear that the signals Earhart was receiving from the boat were becoming fainter and fainter.

Could Earhart and Noonan have made a forced landing on the nearby Phoenix Islands, south of Howland?

Smoke signals

Unable to maintain two-way radio contact, the *Itasca* struggled for nearly six hours to guide the plane towards land. At one point the crew even sent up smoke signals to indicate their position. Finally all contact with the plane was lost. Amelia Earhart, Fred Noonan and the plane were never seen again.

The mystery deepens

For days after Earhart's disappearance, the US naval ships combed the area, but nothing was found. On 4-5 July, distress calls from the plane were picked up by radio operators across the Pacific, but the signals were not strong enough for its position to be pinpointed. Some think Earhart may have mistaken the shadow of a cloud on the water for land and ditched the plane into the sea. Others believe she was captured by the Japanese and held as an American spy. Many have claimed to have found wreckage of the plane, but nothing conclusive has ever been proved. Perhaps we will never know what really happened.

Amelia Earhart at the controls of her plane

What went wrong?

Why did Earhart fail to land on Howland Island? Possible reasons are as follows:

- Neither Earhart nor Noonan were experienced in **radio navigation;**
- The plane and the boat were using **time systems** that were half an hour apart;
- Part of the plane's radio equipment may have been damaged on take-off from New Guinea.

Amelia Earhart's legacy

Over the past 80 years, countless books and articles have been written about Amelia Earhart's disappearance, but the riddle is no closer to being solved. One good outcome from the tragedy is that new ways were found to improve radio communication. These are now followed by ships and pilots all over the world.

The last known photograph of Amelia Earhart and her navigator Fred Noonan with their Lockheed Elektra 10E.

Can YOU solve the mystery?

1 Which theory about Amelia Earhart's disappearance do you think is the most likely? Do some research and make a list of three arguments for and against each theory.

- The plane crashed into the sea and Earhart and Noonan drowned;
- The plane crashed on an island and both survived;
- They were both spies.

2 Which do you think would be the worst place to be lost? Why?

- In a scorching desert;
- In the frozen Antarctic;
- Flying over a snow-capped mountain range;
- In the Amazon rainforest;
- At sea in an open boat;
- In space.

SUPERSONIC HERO

Chuck Yeager and the flight of the Bell X-1

After World War II, the race was on to develop the fastest fighter plane in the world. The world's great superpowers knew that security lay in controlling the skies – and the key to air supremacy was speed.

In the US, the flight research agency NACA had developed a plane that could fly faster than the speed of sound. The trouble was, no pilot was willing to fly it!

Enter Chuck Yeager

One man was to change everything. Born in 1923, Chuck Yeager had earned a reputation during the war as a quick-thinking and fearless fighter pilot. In 1946, he was stationed with the US Airforce at Muroc Airfield, California. With nerves of steel and outstanding flying skills, Yeager was the obvious choice for the supreme challenge in aviation: to test-fly NACA s rocket-powered Bell X-1.

What is the 'sound barrier'?

An Austrian physicist Ernst Mach (1838–1916) first recorded the existence of a 'barrier' created by fast-flying objects. As an aircraft approaches the speed of sound, **shockwaves** build up in front of the plane and create a barrier that is difficult to break through. At the same time, a **vapour cloud** is produced around the aircraft which it appears to fly through.

Chuck Yeager's flying career lasted for over 60 years. He was awarded many medals including the Distinguished Service Medal, the Purple Heart for Bravery and the Presidential Medal of Freedom.

The flying bullet

Like its predecessor, the British de Havilland 108, the design of the Bell X-1 was based on the shape of a 50-calibre bullet – and to fly it at full speed was highly dangerous. But Chuck Yeager was ready for anything. On an early test-flight at Muroc Airfield, shockwaves turned the plane into little more than an unguided missile. Narrowly escaping injury, Yeager managed to land safely and was soon preparing for another attempt.

How fast is 'supersonic'?

The speed of sound, 'Mach 1', varies according to the temperature of the atmosphere – it will be different over hot land and cool water. The speed of sound at sea level is 1,225.1 kph.

Yeager named his plane 'Glamorous Glennis', after his wife. It was painted orange because it was thought it would be easier for the camera and tracker plane to keep sight of it. (In fact, white is a better colour for this.)

Broken ribs

On 12 October 1947, two nights before the flight, Yeager fell off his horse and broke two ribs. Worried that he might not be allowed to fly, he secretly visited a veterinary surgeon in another town and asked to be bandaged up. On the day of the flight he was in such pain that another pilot had to help him climb into the cockpit.

Finally the Bell X-1 was loaded aboard a Boeing 29, taken to a height of 7,000 m and launched. The moment had come. Yeager ignited the rocket chambers and kept accelerating until he had blasted through the sound barrier with over 2,721 kg of **thrust**. He kept going and flew faster than the speed of sound for about 20 seconds before slowing down and landing. The sound barrier had been broken.

> *'I thought I was seeing things! We were flying supersonic! And it was as smooth as a baby's bottom: Grandma could be sitting up there sipping lemonade.'*
>
> Chuck Yeager, on his first supersonic flight

Muroc Airfield (Edwards Air Force Base)

Built on the bed of a vast dry lake, Muroc Airfield, on the edge of California's Mojave Desert, has been home to many of aviation's most important and daring feats, from the test flight of the Bell X-1 (*below*, with crew) to the launch of the US **space shuttles**.

The launch of the space shuttle Columbia *on 12 April 1981*

Muroc Airfield, now renamed Edwards Air Force Base, in California

California
USA
Edwards
Air Force Base

Ball of fire

In 1963, Yeager was test-flying the new Lockheed *Starfighter* at twice the speed of sound when the plane malfunctioned and started to spin out of control. Yeager hit the 'eject' button, but burning debris became caught in his parachute and **pressure suit**. He survived the fall, but needed extensive **skin grafts** before he was back doing what he loved best: flying aeroplanes!

Chuck Yeager's Starfighter bursts into flames in mid-air. Miraculously Yeager himself escaped serious injury.

> '*I got burned pretty bad on my neck and shoulder and it was very difficult to breathe... There is a button on the right, you push it and then you raise your visor. I knew I had to ... get that visor up to shut the oxygen flow from my kit... So I did that. Then I swung a couple times and hit the ground. I couldn't see too much and I was having trouble breathing because there was a lot of smoke and fire. But it worked out... I didn't get killed...*'
>
> Chuck Yeager, on his narrow escape from the blazing Lockheed Starfighter

A 74-year-old Chuck Yeager, photographed on the 50th anniversary of his historic flight in the Bell X-1. After retiring as a test pilot, Yeager joined the Air Force Aerospace Research Pilots' School and trained many of the astronauts in the US Gemini, Mercury and Apollo space programmes.

Could YOU be a test pilot?

1 What part of being a test pilot would appeal to you the most?

- Being a hero;
- Flying some of the fastest planes in the world;
- Doing something no one has ever done before;
- Being rich and famous;
- The danger.

2 Test your memory by answering these questions:

- At what height was the Bell X-1 launched before breaking the sound barrier?
- What colour was the Bell X-1 painted?
- What name did Yeager give to all his planes?
- Was the sound barrier first broken in the USA, the UK or France?

SKY-HIGH ADVENTURE

The record-breaking career of aviator Steve Fossett

On 3 September 2007, the millionaire adventurer Steve Fossett set out for a short flight across the Nevada Desert – and never returned. Despite weeks of searching, his plane, a single-engine Citabria, was never found, and Fossett's fate remains unknown.

Steve Fossett, 1944-2007

Steve Fossett's disappearance made a sad end to a extraordinary career of record-breaking achievements. Born in Tennessee in 1944, Fossett was rarely out of the news. A world-class aviator, he was also the holder of 116 records in sports ranging from swimming, ballooning and motor racing to skiing and mountaineering. Few of his exploits attracted greater attention than his 2005 non-stop, single-handed, round-the-world flight in the spectacular *GlobalFlyer*.

'I do this as a matter of personal satisfaction. To achieve something that is difficult and that stretches my ability to do it.'

Steve Fossett on his career as a record-breaking adventurer

GlobalFlyer at a glance

Built from modern, lightweight materials, *GlobalFlyer* was specially designed to fly non-stop around the world, unrefuelled. The plane's single jet engine was mounted behind the cockpit on the top of the **fuselage**. The huge quantities of fuel needed for the flight were held in 13 containers along the wings. The landing gear was housed in **booms** on either side of the cockpit.

GlobalFlyer: Vital statistics

Wing span	35 m
Wing area	122 sq m
Length	13.44 m
Height	4 m
Gross weight	10 tonnes
Empty weight	1.5 tonnes
Top speed	460+ km/h

Engine mounted behind the cockpit

Fuel tanks in the wings make up 83% of the plane's weight

Drag parachutes stored here to slow the aircraft to landing speed

2-metre long pressurized cockpit. Pilot has to sit on cushions to see out during take-off and landing

Williams **turbo-fan** jet engine uses special fuel with a lower freezing point than standard aviation fuel

GlobalFlyer *on the tarmac at Salina airport, Kansas. Specially designed and built for Fossett's record-breaking flight, the plane was light but strong enough to carry almost six times its own weight in fuel. However, the wings had no protection against ice or sleet, and the plane was not designed for turbulence.*

27

Flying high above the earth

On the morning of 8 February 2005, Steve Fossett attended his final briefing at Salina airport, Kansas, checked the weather reports, squeezed into the tiny cockpit of *GlobalFlyer* and taxied down the runway towards take-off. His attempt on the world's last, great, unbroken aviation record was about to begin.

Flying blind

A few hours into the flight, Fossett suffered his first setback. Due to a technical fault the plane's navigation system shut down. For a time he was flying blind. Fortunately, the system was back in action before he crossed the Atlantic.

Once in the air, Fossett's plan was to fly at an altitude of at least 14 km above the earth's surface – far above the commercial airline traffic and weather systems. With the weight of fuel on board it would take him more than 14 hours to reach this height.

NORTH AMERICA

Salina, Kansas

EUROPE

ASIA

JAPAN

Tokyo

AFRICA

SOUTH AMERICA

After crossing Japan, Fossett's route would take him south to the Equator where the **jet stream** would help carry the plane across the Pacific.

Worse was to come. On the second day, Fossett discovered that 1,200 kg of fuel had been lost due to a fault in the fuel system. Knowing that a forced landing over the Pacific could be fatal, he considered aborting the flight. Then last-minute talks established that the strong tail winds meant he would need less fuel than he had planned. Fossett pressed on.

On 3 March 2005, at 19.50 p.m., Fossett landed *GlobalFlyer* back at Salina, 67 hours, 1 minute and 10 seconds after take-off, having achieved yet another record-breaking flight. He had flown at an average speed of 550.7 kph, making the first solo round-the-world, non-stop, non-refuelled flight.

> 'There was no turning back. It was halfway around the world when I found the fuel problem... Not only might the flight not have finished, but I might have gotten the plane stuck somewhere.'
>
> Steve Fossett

Could YOU be a record-breaker?

1 Imagine you are flying non-stop around the world in *GlobalFlyer*. What do you think would be the worst part of the flight, and why?

    A The cockpit is very small and hot;
    B Turbulence;
    C Not sleeping.

2 What would be the first thing you would say after successfully flying around the world non-stop?

3 After a non-stop, round-the-world flight, what is the first thing you would want to do when you land?

- Go for a long walk;
- Have a slap-up meal;
- Play a video game or watch TV;
- Tell all your friends and have a party.

Glossary

ace a highly skilled person

adrenaline a chemical released in the body when a person is very excited or scared which helps them to react quickly to danger

boom a special container fitted to the wing of an aircraft

canteen a flask for storing water or other drinks

coastguard a person who patrols beaches and looks out for ships or swimmers who need help

decorations medals or badges awarded for bravery in wartime

dogfight a fight between military aircraft in the air

Eiffel Tower a famous tower made out of iron in Paris, France

fixed-wing a type of aircraft with wings attached to the **fuselage**

flare a bright light fired from a gun as a distress signal

fuselage the main body of an aeroplane

high command the top leaders in a military organization

jet stream a current of fast-moving air high in the earth's upper atmosphere

mirage something you think you can see but which isn't really there

Morse code a special 'alphabet' of short and long signals for sending radio messages

NACA the National Advisory Committee for Aeronautics in the USA (replaced in 1958 by the US space agency, NASA)

navigator the person in a plane who plans the journey and guides the pilot

periscope a tube with mirrors, usually used in a submarine to allow the crew to see what is happening on the surface

pressure suit a special suit with an oxygen supply which enables the pilot to breathe when flying at high altitude

radio navigation using radio signals to find out where you are when you are flying a plane or steering a ship

shockwave the force created by build-up of pressure when a plane flies very fast. When the speed of sound is reached, the waves of pressure form a single shockwave.